*W*atched Above, *A*ction Recorded,

*L*ives Reflected

Zabed Mohammad, PhD.

Educator & Educationalist
Canada

Editor
Zarir Muhammad

Rose City Elementary School
Canada

Kids Edu Care, Canada

Printed in Canada and Bangladesh.
For more information, or to book an event, Contact:
www.kidseducare.ca
info@kidseducare.ca
Book design by: Rakibul Islam Tomal
Cover design by: Rakibul Islam Tomal
ISBN - Paperback: 978-1-998923-79-3
ISBN – Hardcover: 978-1-998923-78-6
ISBN – E-book: 978-1-998923-77-9
First Edition: May 2025

Author's Note

Oh Teens, Youth, Young Minds!

Have you ever felt like no one is watching you? Like you could do something in secret—hidden from the eyes of your parents, siblings, teachers, friends, or even the law? You might feel clever, as though you're outsmarting the world around you.

But remember—there is One who sees everything. No one can hide anything from His sight. And who is that One? It is God—Allah (SWT), the Almighty.

I remind myself of this universal truth often. It humbles me to know that my actions—just like yours—are always seen, always recorded, and will be accounted for on the Day of Judgment. We may hide from human eyes, but we can never hide from the eyes of God/Allah (SWT).

This book is a call to reflection—a reminder that our actions in this life shape our eternity. Like you, I must strive to live with justice, honesty, kindness, and a deep awareness that we are always being watched from above.

Sometimes, while driving or walking past a graveyard, I find myself reflecting on those who have already completed their worldly journey. In these moments, I remember my own parents—my beloved father, whom I lost in childhood, and my dear mother, who passed away in 2019. When they were alive, they loved me deeply. And like me, I invite you — our readers — to reflect on your own loved ones who have departed.

No matter how advanced our technology becomes — no matter how intelligent or powerful we are — we cannot reach out to them. We can send messages across continents in seconds using our phones, yet we cannot connect with those who are just a few feet beneath the earth — five feet three inches, or 63 inches, or 160.2 centimeters below.

We may assume they are in Paradise. We can pray for them, since they can no longer perform good deeds. They are so close in distance, yet entirely beyond our reach.

When they were alive, they may have been stronger than us, more successful, or enjoyed life in ways we only dream of today. But now, their worldly chapter is closed, and they have entered the eternal phase.

As our divine books remind us, there are only two destinations in the afterlife: Paradise and Hell. Paradise is not for the clever tricksters or those who merely "get away" with wrongdoing. It is reserved for those who choose righteousness — even when no one is watching.

So think. Reflect. Look back on your life. This world is temporary — 50, 60, maybe even 100 years. But the life to come? It is eternal...

Let us attempt together — for the reward that lasts forever.

— **Zabed Mohammad, PhD**

Contents

Dedication

To the **teens, youth,** and **young adults** of today and
tomorrow —
A gentle reminder that
*every action we take is recorded, nothing
is ever erased, and nothing remains
hidden.*
May this awareness guide us toward universal truth,
integrity, and a life of purpose.

Part: 1

The Gathering Begins

The soft glow of the setting sun filtered through the large windows of the community center, casting a warm light over the circle of chairs in the middle of the room. The hum of excited chatter filled the air as a group of teens, each from different backgrounds, gathered with curiosity in their eyes. This evening wasn't just any regular meeting — it was an evening to discuss the big questions: **life and purpose, daily activities, and faith.**

At the center of the circle stood Brother Raef. Calm, composed, and approachable, he had a gentle presence that drew people in. It wasn't because he was particularly tall or imposing, but because of the sincerity he radiated. Brother Raef was a Hafiz-e-Al-Quran, someone who had memorized the entire Al-Quran, but despite his deep knowledge, he remained humble and relatable, especially to teens.

He clapped his hands gently, signaling the start of the session. The chatter quieted, and all eyes turned to him.

"Welcome, everyone," he began, his voice warm and welcoming. "I'm glad you're here. This space is for you—a space to ask questions, share your thoughts, and explore what it means to live a meaningful life. No question is too big or too small. Feel free to ask whatever is on your mind."

The teens exchanged glances. Some were eager to dive in, while others seemed unsure. Among them were Sarah, a girl who loved to debate; Ahmad, a quiet boy who often kept his thoughts to himself; Liam, who often questioned authority and called himself an atheist; and Aisha, a shy girl who often found herself stuck between faith and doubt.

Brother Raef continued, "I know that some of you believe in God/Allah (SWT), some of you don't, and some of you are just curious. Whatever your journey is, I respect it, and I'm happy you're here."

Sarah was the first to speak up, her voice sharp with curiosity. "Brother Raef, you said we can ask anything, right?"

"Absolutely," he said, nodding with a smile.

She leaned forward, her eyes focused. "How can you believe in something you can't see? God/Allah (SWT), angels, all of that—it just feels like stories made up to control people."

A few heads nodded in agreement. Liam smiled, clearly enjoying the challenge. Ahmad shifted in his seat, uncomfortable, and Aisha lowered her head, unsure how to respond.

Brother Raef didn't seem bothered. "That's a great question, Sarah. And we'll get into that. But before we do, let me share a story."

The group fell silent, intrigued.

"There was once a traveler," he began, his voice calm and steady. "He was walking through a vast desert, the sun beating down on him. As he walked, he noticed footprints in the sand. He didn't see the person who made them, but he knew someone had passed that way. He didn't question it—he simply accepted that the footprints were evidence of a traveler. In the same way, we might not see Allah directly, but we can see His signs everywhere—whether it's the way the universe is designed, the way our bodies heal, or even the emotions we feel."

The teens sat in silence, taking in his words.

Liam broke the silence with a sarcastic laugh. "Okay, footprints are easy to spot. But what signs are you talking about? The universe? That's just science, not God/Allah (SWT)."

Brother Raef chuckled softly, unbothered by Liam's skepticism. "Good point, Liam. Let's explore that. But first, let me ask all of you this: Have you ever done something that you thought no one saw, only to feel like... maybe someone did?"

The room fell quiet. Sarah tilted her head, interested but cautious. Liam crossed his arms, as though daring Raef to convince him. Ahmad looked up for the first time, making eye contact with Raef, while Aisha gave a small nod, her cheeks turning pink.

Raef leaned in a little, lowering his voice, almost like sharing a secret. "What if I told you that everything you've ever done — every action, every word, every thought — is being recorded? Not by cameras or people, but by two noble beings who are with you all the time. Would that change how you see yourself? Would it change your choices?"

The teens were captivated now, their curiosity piqued.

Sarah was the first to speak. "You mean... angels?"

"Yes," Raef replied simply, his tone calm but firm. "They don't just watch. They write. Every good deed, every mistake, every intention is recorded by them. They're with us, though we can't see them."

Liam raised his hand, a skeptical smirk on his face. "Sorry, but that sounds like something out of a fantasy novel. Angels on our shoulders? Writing everything down? Where's the proof?"

Brother Raef smiled without missing a beat. "That's a great question, Liam. Let me share what the Al-Quran says about this." He paused, giving everyone a moment.

In Chapter/*Surah Qamar: 54, Verse: 52, it says, "and indeed, the record of the wicked is in sijjin."* And in Chapter/*Surah Infitar: 82, Verses: 10-12), "and indeed, over you are appointed angels, noble and recording, who know what you do."*

So yes, according to the Al-Quran, everything we do is recorded by angels."

Liam shifted in his seat, thinking. Sarah, looking a bit more thoughtful now, asked, "Okay, but why would God/Allah (SWT) do that? Why not just show us everything clearly? If God/Allah (SWT) is real, why doesn't He just prove it to everyone?"

Brother Raef nodded thoughtfully, as if anticipating the question. "That's an important question, Sarah. And it's something that many people wonder.

The Al-Quran gives us a challenge in Chapter/Surah Al-Baqarah: 2, Verse: 23: "and if you are in doubt about what we have sent down upon our servant [Muhammad], then produce a Chapter/surah the like thereof..."

Allah challenges people to provide evidence, to prove what they claim. But the reality is, belief isn't about seeing everything clearly; it's about faith in the unseen, which is actually a strength."

Aisha spoke up for the first time, her voice soft but clear. "So, faith is about trusting in something you can't always see?"

"Exactly," Brother Raef said, smiling warmly at Aisha. "Faith is about trusting in what's real, even when you can't see it with your eyes. It's about knowing that there's a greater purpose behind everything, even if we don't always understand it."

The room was silent for a moment, as the teens processed his words.

Finally, Ahmad spoke up, his voice quieter than usual. "So, you're saying that even if I can't see angels, or see God/Allah (SWT), the fact that I believe in them... that still matters?"

Raef nodded. "Yes, Ahmad. Belief in the unseen, and living according to that belief, is powerful. It shapes how you see the world and how you live your life."

There was a pause as the teens reflected on what had been said. Raef stood up, signaling that their time was almost up.

"Before we close," he said, "I want to leave you with one last thought: Everything you do, every choice you make, is recorded. And one day, you will be shown all of it — good or bad. But that doesn't have to scare you. It's an opportunity. An opportunity to live with intention, to choose good, and to know that you are being watched by angels, and by Allah, who is always merciful and just."

The group sat quietly, thinking about the idea of being watched, of angels recording their actions, and of the challenge of faith. The night had only just begun, and it was clear that many more questions were on the way.

"Are you ready for the next part?" Raef asked, his smile gentle but encouraging.

The teens nodded, their minds now open to exploring more.

"Food For Thought"

Q. 1. How does believing in angels change the way we act?

Q. 2. Is knowing that our actions are recorded scary or helpful? Why?

Q. 3. How is God/Allah (SWT)'s watchfulness different from cameras and technology?

Q. 4. Can faith and science work together? Why or why not?

Q. 5. If your actions were recorded and shown to you, would you change anything?

Reflections of the Heart: What Did You Take In?

Q. 1. Why did Brother Raef share the story about footprints in the desert?

A. To illustrate how unseen things can be recognized through signs.

B. To prove science is unreliable.

C. To explain how we can see angels.

D. To entertain the teens with a parable.

Answer:....?

Q. 2. What does Surah Infitar (82:10-12) say about angels?

A. Angels protect us from all harm.

B. Angels appear to people in dreams.

C. Angels are appointed to record everything we do

D. Angels are only symbolic in Islam.

Answer:....?

Q. 3. How did Brother Raef describe the concept of faith?

A. A blind belief in stories.

B. Trusting in what we cannot always see.

C. Something that only religious scholars need.

D. Belief based solely on emotions.

Answer:....?

Q. 4. How did the teens initially react to the idea of angels recording their actions?

A. They all believed it immediately.

B. They ignored Brother Raef's words.

C. They showed mixed feelings — some skeptical, others curious.

D. They left the room in confusion

Answer:....?

Q. 5. What was Brother Raef's main message at the end of the session?

A. Fear Allah because everything is recorded.

B. Everything will be forgotten, so live freely.

C. Life is meaningless without proof.

D. Live with intention, knowing that your actions are seen and recorded.

Answer:....?

Part: 2

Who is Watching Us?

The room was buzzing with curiosity, and a sense of excitement filled the air. Brother Raef looked around at the teens seated in front of him, sensing their mix of doubt and genuine interest. Liam was leaning back in his chair with his arms crossed, his eyes challenging Raef to explain things that made sense. Sarah sat forward, her chin resting in her hand, ready to ask another question. Ahmad was quietly attentive, and Aisha nervously fidgeted with the sleeve of her shirt, deep in thought.

Raef began, his voice calm and steady. "Let's start with a simple but deep question: Who is watching us?"

The teens exchanged uncertain glances. Sarah was the first to speak up. "You mean Allah, right? But how can He be watching us if we can't see Him?"

"That's exactly what we're going to explore," Raef replied with a smile. "Let me start by sharing a verse from the Al-Quran.

God/Allah says: 'And He is with you wherever you are (Chapter/Surah Al-Hadid: 57, Verse: 4)."

He paused, allowing the words to sink in.

Liam snorted. "Okay, but what does that even mean? Is Allah literally everywhere? And why can't we see Him if He's always watching us?"

Raef nodded, acknowledging Liam's doubt. "Great questions, Liam. Let's break it down. When Allah says He is with us, it doesn't mean He's physically next to us. Allah's presence and knowledge are beyond time and space. He sees, hears, and knows everything. It's like the wind—you can't see it, but you can feel it and know it's there. In the same way, we may not see Allah, but we can recognize His signs—like the way the sun rises or the way our hearts beat without us thinking about it. These are signs of Allah's presence."

Sarah raised her eyebrow. "But if He's everywhere and knows everything, why doesn't He just show Himself? Wouldn't it be easier for people to believe?"

Raef leaned forward, his tone gentle but firm. "That's another great question. Allah answers this in the Al-Quran.

In Surah Al-An'am: 6, Verse: 103, He says: "Vision perceives Him not, but He perceives [all] vision; and He is the Subtle, the Acquainted."

Our human senses are limited. Just like we can't look directly at the sun without hurting our eyes, we can't perceive Allah with our senses because He is beyond our understanding."

The room fell quiet. The teens were thinking about this, trying to grasp the idea. Liam, however, wasn't finished. "Okay, but if He's watching us all the time, isn't that… creepy? Why does He need to watch everything we do?"

Raef chuckled softly, easing the tension in the room. "I understand why it might feel that way, but let me explain. Think about it like this: Imagine you're in a school play, and your parents are in the audience. They're watching you not to judge you, but because they love you and want to see you do well. Allah's watching is not about control or judgment — it's about His care and guidance. He watches over us because He wants the best for us, to guide us toward good choices and help us avoid harm."

Aisha spoke up for the first time, her voice soft. "But what if we make mistakes? Does that mean He's always disappointed in us?"

Raef's expression softened. "That's a beautiful question, Aisha. Allah knows we're not perfect. He created us with free will, and He knows we'll make mistakes. What's important is that we recognize our mistakes and try to do better.

In Chapter/Surah Az-Zumar: 39, Verse: 53, Allah says: "Say, O My servants who have wronged yourselves [by sinning], do not despair of the mercy of Allah. Indeed, Allah forgives all sins. He is the Forgiving, the Merciful.' So, even when we slip up, His mercy is always there to pick us up."

The teens fell silent, reflecting on what Raef had said. Ahmad, who had been quiet until now, spoke up. "So, if He's always watching us, does that mean we should always try to do the right thing?"

Raef smiled warmly. "Exactly, Ahmad. Knowing that Allah is watching us reminds us to be mindful of our actions. It's not about fear — it's about responsibility. Imagine you're playing a video game, and every move you make is being recorded for your final score. Wouldn't you try to play your best? In the same way, our lives are being recorded — not just by Allah, but also by two angels who are with us, writing down everything we do, good and bad."

Liam raised an eyebrow, unconvinced. "But that sounds like a way to control people. What if I don't care about being watched? What if I just want to live my life?"

Raef's gaze softened. "Liam, you have the freedom to choose how you want to live. That's the beauty of free will. But let me ask you this: If you knew someone was watching over you, not to control you, but to guide and protect you, wouldn't that change how you see things? Allah's watching is not about control—it's about giving us a chance to grow, reflect, and become the best versions of ourselves."

The room was quiet, and even Liam seemed to be considering the idea. Raef leaned back in his chair, giving the teens time to reflect. "Let's keep this conversation going. Next, we'll talk about the two angels on our shoulders—who they are and what they do. But for now, think about this: What would you do differently if you truly believed someone was always there to guide you, protect you, and help you become the best version of yourself?"

The teens were quiet, but it was clear their curiosity was growing. Even if they didn't admit it, they were beginning to think deeper about their choices and actions.

"Food For Thought"

Q. 1. How is God/Allah (SWT)'s watchfulness different from being watched by technology?

Q. 2. Does not seeing Allah make it harder to believe in Him? Why or why not?

Q. 3. How does knowing Allah is watching affect the way we behave?

Q. 4. Does believing in divine accountability make life easier or harder?

Q. 5. How can this discussion help us make better choices in daily life?

Comprehension Check: Exploring Belief and Meaning

Q. 1. What does the verse from Chapter/Surah Al-Hadid (57:4) emphasize about Allah?

A. That Allah is physically present with us

B. That Allah is with us wherever we are

C. That Allah is always watching through angels

D. That Allah appears to people in visions

Answer:….?

Q. 2. How did Brother Raef describe Allah's presence to help the teens understand it?

A. As something we can see in dreams

B. Like a teacher observing a classroom

C. Like the wind — unseen but felt

D. Like a parent scolding a child

Answer:....?

Q. 3. According to chapter/Surah Al-An'am (6:103), why can't we see Allah?

A. Because He hides Himself from people

B. Because He only reveals Himself to prophets

C. Because He lives in a different realm

D. Because our vision is too weak to perceive Him

Answer:....?

Q. 4. Why did Brother Raef compare Allah's watchfulness to parents watching a school play?

A. To show that Allah is judging everything we do

B. To show that Allah watches us out of love and care

C. To help the teens feel more afraid

D. To explain that Allah is spying on us

Answer:....?

Q. 5. What message does Chapter/Surah Az-Zumar (39:53) convey?

A. That people are judged strictly with no forgiveness

B. That angels decide who gets forgiven

C. That Allah forgives all sins if we turn to Him

D. That only good people are loved by Allah

Answer:....?

Part: 3

The Role of Angels: Fact or Fiction?

The group gathered again, the conversation from the previous night still fresh in their minds. Brother Raef noticed the mixture of curiosity and skepticism in their faces. Liam sat with his arms crossed, a skeptical look on his face, while Sarah was ready with her notebook, pen in hand. Aisha seemed thoughtful, and Ahmad looked like he had questions he was eager to ask.

Raef smiled. "Tonight, we're going to talk about something very interesting: the role of angels, especially the two who record our actions, the **Kiraman Katibin**."

Liam raised his hand dramatically. "Wait, so you're saying there are real angels sitting on our shoulders, writing down everything we do? That sounds like a fantasy story."

The room chuckled, but Raef stayed calm. "I know it might sound like a fairy tale, but let's take a closer look at what the Al-Quran says.

Allah (SWT) tells us in Chapter/Surah Al-Infitar: 82, Verses: 10-12, "Indeed, over you are appointed keepers, noble and recording; they know whatever you do."

The angels are recording our actions for accountability. On the Day of Judgment, Allah will show us our deeds, and these records will speak for or against us.

Allah (SWT) says in Chapter/Surah Al-Kahf: 18, Verse: 49, "The record [of deeds] will be placed open, and you will see the criminals fearful of that within it."

Sarah raised her hand. "But how do we know this is true? Couldn't this just be a metaphor for our conscience?"

"That's a great question, Sarah," Raef replied. "The Al-Quran speaks of angels as real, created beings with specific duties. For example,

In Chapter/Surah Qaaf: 50, Verse: 17, it says, "When the two receivers receive, seated on the right and on the left."

This verse clearly describes the angels' positions, meaning they are not just ideas — they are real beings with a job to do: recording our actions. Yes, they are always with us, recording both our good and bad deeds. This is not to control us but to remind us to live righteously, as-

Allah says in Chapter/Surah Al-Infitar: 82, Verses: 10-12, "Indeed, over you are appointed keepers, noble and recording; they know whatever you do."

Aisha shifted in her seat, looking concerned. "But how can they possibly record everything we do? We do so much every day."

Raef nodded, understanding her concern. "It does seem impossible, right? But think about this: technology today can track and store massive amounts of data. Your phone tracks your location, records your voice, and even recognizes your face. If humans can create devices like this, imagine what Allah, the Creator of everything, can do. Angels are not limited by human technology or understanding — they can record everything perfectly."

Liam shrugged. "Okay, let's say these angels are real. But why would they bother recording everything? What's the point?"

Raef smiled gently. "The purpose is accountability. Think of it like a school exam. Every test you take is recorded by the teacher, not to control you, but to help you understand where you can improve. The angels' role is to record your deeds — good and bad. On the Day of Judgment, we will see everything we've done, and these records will speak for or against us.

Allah says in Chapter/Surah Al-Kahf: 18, Verse: 49, "And the record [of deeds] will be placed open, and you will see the criminals fearful of that within it. And they will say, 'Oh, woe to us! What is this book that leaves nothing small or great except that it has enumerated it?"

Sarah's face showed concern. "But isn't that scary? Knowing that every mistake we make is recorded?"

Raef's voice softened. "It can feel overwhelming, but remember, the same system records your good deeds too, even the smallest ones.

Allah says in Chapter/Surah Az-Zalzalah: 99, Verses: 7-8, "So whoever does an atom's weight of good will see it, and whoever does an atom's weight of evil will see it."

The angels are fair — they record everything, and Allah judges with perfect justice and mercy."

Ahmad, who had been quiet up until now, spoke up. "But how can we know angels even exist? We can't see them."

Raef smiled, a familiar question. "Good point, Ahmad. Do you believe in gravity?"

Ahmad nodded. "Of course."

"Can you see gravity?"

"No, but we can see its effects," Ahmad replied, starting to understand.

"Exactly," Raef said. "We believe in many things we can't see because we see their effects. Angels are part of the unseen world that Allah has created. Just because we can't see them doesn't mean they don't exist.

In Chapter/Surah Al-Baqarah: 2, Verse: 3, Allah reminds us that true believers are those "who believe in the unseen.' Belief in the unseen is an act of faith."

Liam leaned in, his curiosity piqued. "But why make it so complicated? Why not just show us the angels or let them speak to us?"

Raef's expression grew serious. "Liam, if we could see angels, it would remove the test of faith. This life is a test to see who believes in the unseen, who trusts in Allah even when they can't see Him or His angels. Faith is about doing good because it's the right thing, not because we're being watched. Angels remind us that nothing escapes Allah's knowledge."

The room grew quiet, everyone deep in thought. Even Liam seemed to be considering the idea.

Raef leaned back, letting the words settle in. "I know this is a lot to think about, but let me leave you with a question: If you knew everything you did was being recorded, how would it change the way you live your life?"

"Food For Thought"

Q. 1. Do you think angels recording our actions is similar to technology tracking us? Why or why not?

Q. 2. How does knowing our actions are recorded make us more responsible?

Q. 3. If we knew for sure that the afterlife exists, how would we live differently?

Q. 4. Can faith and science work together to help us understand life and the hereafter?

Q. 5. What was the most thought-provoking idea from today's discussion?

Think Fast, Reflect Deep: What's Your Take?

Q. 1. According to Chapter/Surah Al-Infitar (82:10-12), what is the primary role of the Kiraman Katibin?

A. To record all actions of humans

B. To guide humans to Paradise

C. To protect humans from evil

D. To deliver messages to prophets.

Answer:.....?

Q. 2. How does Raef explain the ability of angels to record everything we do?

A. By comparing them to mythical beings

B. By highlighting their use of human technology

C. By comparing them to modern devices that track data

D. By saying they use human assistants

Answer:.....?

Q. 3. Why, according to Raef, are humans not shown angels during their lifetime?

A. Because angels are afraid of humans

B. Because it would remove the test of faith

C. Because humans are not pure enough

D. Because angels are invisible to everyone

Correct Answer: C. Because it would remove the test of faith

Answer:.....?

Q. 4. What is the significance of Chapter/Surah Az-Zalzalah (99:7-8) as discussed in the story?

A. It promises immediate punishment for bad deeds

B. It shows that only major sins are recorded

C. It emphasizes that even the smallest deeds are

recorded

D. It proves angels are physically present

Answer:....?

Q. 5. What analogy does Raef use to help Ahmad understand the existence of angels?

A. Electricity

B. The internet

C. Wind

D. Gravity

Answer:....?

Part: 4

The Purpose of Creation: Why Are We Here?

As the evening sky grew darker, the teens gathered in a quiet room, and Brother Raef noticed the eager, yet thoughtful expressions on their faces. He knew that tonight's topic would stir up big questions — questions everyone eventually wonders about: "Why are we here? What is our purpose?"

"Tonight's topic is one that everyone, at some point, thinks about," Brother Raef began, speaking gently. "Why are we here? What is our purpose? Let's begin with what the Al-Quran teaches us."

The teens were quiet, ready to dive into the conversation. Sarah, who often had tough questions, raised her hand.

"I've heard a lot about worshipping Allah, but I don't fully understand," Sarah said. "Why are we here? What does Allah really want from us?"

Brother Raef smiled kindly at Sarah. "That's a question we all have. The Al-Quran makes it very clear.

In Chapter/Surah Adh-Dhariyat: 51, Verse 56, Allah says, "And I did not create the jinn and mankind except to worship Me."

So, our main purpose in life is to worship Allah. But what does that really mean?"

Liam, confused, scratched his head. "Wait, worship? Does that mean we have to spend our whole lives praying all the time? Isn't there more to life than just praying?"

Raef chuckled softly. "Good question, Liam! Worship isn't only about praying five times a day. Worship in Islam means anything that brings you closer to Allah. It's about living in a way that follows Allah's guidance. So, when you are kind to others, help someone in need, or even study to gain knowledge—these are all ways you can worship Allah."

Aisha, deep in thought, nodded. "So, worship isn't just about praying?"

"Exactly, Aisha," Raef replied. "It's how we live each moment. Worship is in everything we do, as long as it's done in a way that pleases Allah."

Sarah, curious again, asked, "But what if someone doesn't believe in Allah? What if they don't worship Him? What's their purpose?"

Brother Raef paused, choosing his words carefully. "That's an important question, Sarah. Everyone has the choice to believe or not. But Allah created us to recognize Him as the Creator and worship Him. If someone doesn't believe in Allah, they are missing the very purpose they were made for. It's not that Allah punishes them for their disbelief, but they are simply not fulfilling their true purpose."

Liam raised his eyebrows, "But what about people who do good things? They help others, they are kind, but they don't believe in God/Allah (SWT). Is that enough?"

"That's a great question, Liam," Brother Raef answered thoughtfully. "Doing good deeds is important. Allah loves kindness and goodness. But the foundation of every good deed is recognizing Allah.

In Chapter/Surah Al-Baqarah: 2, Verse: 177, Allah says, "It is not righteousness that you turn your faces toward the East or the West, but righteousness is in one who believes in Allah, the Last Day, the Angels, the Book, and the Prophets..."

This verse shows that true goodness begins with believing in Allah and living by His guidance."

Aisha, understanding more now, asked, "So, believing in Allah isn't just about saying 'I believe.' It's about living by that belief every day, right?"

"Exactly," Raef said, smiling. "Belief in Allah isn't just something you say with your words. It's something you show in everything you do—your actions, how you treat others, how you live with purpose."

Liam still had a question, "But what about people who've never heard of Allah or people who don't have the chance to learn about Him? What happens to them?"

Raef nodded thoughtfully. "This is an important point. Allah is the Most Just, and He will never punish anyone without giving them a fair chance to know the truth. Many people in the world might never hear about Islam or know about Allah. But it's not for us to judge anyone's fate. Allah knows everyone's heart, and He will judge fairly. Our job as believers is to share the message of Islam through our words and actions, not to judge others."

Aisha raised her hand again, now understanding a bigger picture. "So, our purpose isn't just about believing in Allah; it's also about helping others find their purpose too?"

Raef's eyes brightened. "Exactly, Aisha. One of the best things we can do as Muslims is to share the message of Allah—not just with our words, but by showing others through our actions. When we live with faith, we are fulfilling the reason we were created—to worship Allah and help others do the same."

The teens sat in silence for a moment, reflecting on what they had just learned. Sarah spoke up, with a clearer understanding in her voice. "I think I get it now. We were created to live with purpose—to worship Allah in everything we do. And even if we don't always get it perfect, Allah is always there, guiding us and giving us chances to do better."

Brother Raef smiled warmly. "Exactly, Sarah. Life is about striving to fulfill your purpose, doing your best, and always seeking Allah's guidance. Allah knows your heart, and He is always there to guide you, as long as you sincerely seek Him."

As the night ended, the teens felt a deeper sense of understanding. They were no longer just asking questions—they were beginning to find answers within themselves. Bit by bit, they were starting to see the bigger picture: the purpose of life, the importance of faith, and how they could live with purpose and meaning.

"Food For Thought"

Q. 1. What is the main purpose of our creation, according to Brother Raef?

Q. 2. How can we worship Allah in our daily lives, beyond just praying?

Q. 3. What happens to people who don't believe in Allah or haven't heard about Him?

Q. 4. Why is it important to show our belief in Allah through our actions?

Q. 5. What does it mean to live with purpose and how can we help others find their purpose?

Challenge Yourself: What Do You Remember?

Q. 1. According to Brother Raef, what is the main purpose of our creation as mentioned in the Quran?

A. To explore the world

B. To help others

C. To worship Allah

D. To gain knowledge

Answer:.....?

Q. 2. What does Brother Raef explain about the meaning of worship in Islam?

A. It only refers to praying five times a day

B. It is limited to performing rituals

C. It includes all actions done to please Allah

D. It means avoiding all fun and entertainment

Answer:.....?

Q. 3. How did Brother Raef respond to the question about people who are kind but don't believe in Allah?

A. He said they are better than believers

B. He emphasized that good deeds without belief miss the core purpose

C. He said belief doesn't matter as long as you are kind

D. He said Allah doesn't care about belief

Answer:.....?

Q. 4. What does Chapter/Surah Al-Baqarah, verse 177, highlight as the foundation of righteousness?

A. Following cultural traditions

B. Praying towards the East or West

C. Belief in Allah and living by His guidance

D. Being generous to family only

Answer:....?

Q. 5. According to the discussion, how can Muslims help others find their purpose in life?

A. By debating with others

B. By judging people for their choices

C. By living with faith and showing good actions

D. By avoiding people with different beliefs

Answer:....?

Part: 5

Free Will and Accountability

The evening's discussion had been flowing for a while, and the teens were listening attentively, each one eager to understand more. Brother Raef could sense that the group was beginning to understand the significance of their connection with Allah, but there was still one major question to tackle. He paused for a moment, sensing that it was time to address a deeper topic.

"Today, we'll talk about something that many people find confusing—free will and accountability. It's a question that can make you think a lot. Some people ask, 'If Allah knows everything, if He has already decided everything for us, do we really have free will? Are we still responsible for what we do?'"

The teens looked at each other, unsure of how to respond. Finally, Liam spoke, his voice filled with doubt, "But isn't it true that God/Allah (SWT) already knows everything that will happen? So, how can we be free if everything is already decided?"

Brother Raef nodded thoughtfully. "That's a very good question, Liam. It's a question that has troubled many people. But the truth is, Allah's knowledge of everything — past, present, and future — doesn't take away our ability to choose. Allah's knowledge is different from our understanding. He knows what we will choose, but He doesn't force us to make those choices."

Sarah, still unsure, asked, "But if we are free to choose, then why does it sometimes feel like things are out of our control? Like when bad things happen, it feels like it's not our fault."

Raef smiled gently, understanding her concern. "You're right, Sarah. Life can feel like that sometimes. But what you need to understand is that Allah gives us free will to make choices. The outcomes of our choices, however, are not always in our hands. This is where accountability comes in."

He opened his Al-Quran and read a verse aloud:

"And whatever good befalls you, it is from Allah; and whatever evil befalls you, it is from yourself." (Chapter/Surah An-Nisa: 4:, Verse: 79)

Raef continued, "Allah gives us the freedom to choose. When something good happens, it's a blessing from Him. But when things go wrong or we make mistakes, it's often the result of our own choices. Allah doesn't make us choose bad things. He gives us the freedom, and with that freedom comes the responsibility for our actions."

Liam looked unconvinced. "So, you're saying that even though Allah knows what will happen, He still gives us the choice?"

"Yes, exactly," Raef replied. "Allah's knowledge doesn't take away your freedom to choose. It's like a teacher who knows how a student will do on a test, based on their preparation, but still lets the student take the test. The teacher doesn't choose the grade; it's based on the student's choices during the test."

Aisha raised her hand, looking thoughtful. "But what if something really bad happens to us, like an accident or something we couldn't control? How is that our fault?"

Raef's expression softened with understanding. "Life is full of challenges, Aisha, and not all bad things happen because of our own choices. Sometimes bad things happen because of other people's actions, or because of circumstances beyond our control. But even in those situations, Allah asks us to remain patient, trust in His wisdom, and try to do good despite the difficulties.

Allah says in the Al-Quran:

"Do not kill yourselves. Indeed, Allah is ever merciful to you." (Chapter/Surah An-Nisa: 4, Verse: 29)

Allah doesn't want us to lose hope but to face difficulties with strength and faith."

Sarah leaned forward, her voice filled with curiosity. "So, even if we can't control what happens to us, we're still responsible for how we react?"

"Exactly," Brother Raef said. "We may not be able to control everything that happens to us, but we can control how we respond. How we react to challenges, the choices we make during those moments, and the way we treat others—all of that is what Allah holds us accountable for."

Liam, still puzzled, asked, "But if Allah already knows everything that will happen, what's the point of making choices? Doesn't it all just end up being part of a plan?"

Raef took a deep breath and smiled. "That's a great question, Liam. Allah's knowledge doesn't make us robots. He gives us free will so that we can choose to follow the right path. The beauty of our choices lies in our ability to choose to do what's right. Allah gives us opportunities every day to make good choices, and He rewards us for those choices."

Aisha thought for a moment and then asked, "So we are still responsible for our actions, even if Allah already knows what we're going to do?"

"Yes," Brother Raef said. "It's like a person writing a story. The author knows how the story will end, but the characters in the story are still making choices that lead to that ending. Allah knows how our story will end, but He lets us live it out through our own choices."

Sarah nodded slowly. "I think I get it now. We have the freedom to make choices, but we're also responsible for those choices. And even if things don't always go our way, it's up to us to stay patient and keep trying to do the right thing."

"Exactly, Sarah," Raef said with a warm smile. "Allah doesn't expect us to control everything. He asks us to strive for good, make choices that please Him, and trust that He knows what's best for us. Our task is to use our free will wisely, and that's what we'll be accountable for."

The teens sat in silence, thinking deeply about the conversation. They weren't overwhelmed anymore; they felt a sense of purpose. They still had questions, but they had taken a step toward understanding their role in this world.

Brother Raef looked around the room with a sense of satisfaction. "In the end, we are all given this beautiful gift of free will. It's what we choose to do with it that matters. And no matter where we are in life, we can always turn to Allah for guidance."

As the evening came to a close, the teens felt more grounded in the knowledge that they were accountable for their choices, and that Allah's mercy was always there to guide them.

"Food For Thought"

Q. 1. What is the difference between Allah's knowledge and our free will?

Q. 2. Why is it important to take responsibility for our actions, even when bad things happen?

Q. 3. How does Allah want us to react when we face challenges or difficulties?

Q. 4. If Allah knows everything that will happen, why do we still have to make choices?

Q. 5. What does it mean to use our free will wisely, and why is it important for our accountability?

"Faith in Focus: Check Your Understanding"

Q. 1. What does Brother Raef say about Allah's knowledge and our free will?

A. Allah's knowledge forces us to make certain choices

B. Allah's knowledge means we have no control over our lives

C. Allah knows what we will choose, but we still have the freedom to make those choices

D. Allah only knows our good choices, not our

Answer:....?

Q. 2. According to Al-Quran 4:79, what is the source of the evil that befalls us?

A. Our own choices

B. Satan

C. Other people's decisions

D. The environment around us

Answer:....?

Q. 3. How does Brother Raef explain our reaction to events we cannot control, like accidents?

A. We are not accountable in any way

B. We should question Allah's plan

C. We are accountable for how we respond to such events

D. We should avoid all risks

Answer:....?

Q. 4. Why does Brother Raef compare Allah's knowledge to a teacher knowing how a student will perform?

A. To show that teachers control students' grades

B. To prove that tests are unfair

C. To suggest Allah gives tests that we cannot pass

D. To explain that foreknowledge doesn't remove free will

Answer:....?

Q. 5. What does using our free will wisely mean in the context of accountability?

A. Doing whatever feels right in the moment

B. Ignoring consequences and trusting fate

C. Choosing actions that please Allah and accepting responsibility

D. Letting others decide for us

Answer:....?

Part: 6

Evidence of Faith in a Skeptical World

As the conversation continued, Brother Raef noticed that the teens were starting to question not only big ideas about life but also the very foundation of their beliefs. There was a mix of curiosity and doubt in the room, as they wrestled with some of the hardest questions about faith and existence.

Finally, Layla, who had been quiet until then, spoke up. "I don't get it," she said, sounding confused. "Why doesn't Allah just show Himself to everyone? If He exists, why doesn't He make it clear, like right in front of our eyes?"

Brother Raef paused for a moment, choosing his words carefully. He knew this was one of the most common and difficult questions people had about faith.

"Layla, that's a question many people have asked throughout history," he began gently. "It's not a new question, and it's a good one. But here's the thing: Allah doesn't want us to believe in Him because we see Him directly. What He wants is for us to believe from our hearts, through our understanding, and by reflecting on the signs He has already given us."

He opened the Al-Quran to a verse that he had always found powerful.

"And if you are in doubt about what We have sent down upon Our Servant [Muhammad], then produce a surah the like thereof..." (Chapter/Surah Al-Baqarah: 2, Verse: 23).

"This verse is a challenge from Allah to anyone who doubts the truth of the Al-Quran. Allah is saying, 'If you think this Al-Quran is not from Me, then try to bring something like it — something that can match its beauty, wisdom, and guidance. If you can't, then know that it is from Allah.'"

Liam, who had been skeptical so far, leaned forward. "But if God/Allah (SWT) is so powerful, why doesn't He just make it obvious? Why all this mystery?"

Brother Raef smiled kindly. "It's not a mystery, Liam. It's a test. Imagine if Allah just appeared to everyone. People would have no choice but to believe. It would be like walking into a room and seeing the answer to a math problem written on the board. There would be no challenge, no choice involved. Faith would lose its meaning because it would be based on sight, not belief. Allah wants us to believe in Him even when we can't see Him directly, and that is what makes our faith meaningful."

Layla looked puzzled. "But doesn't that make it hard for people to believe? If they don't see Allah, how can they know for sure He's real?"

"That's a good question, Layla," Brother Raef replied. "Yes, it's not always easy. But think about this: We don't see air, yet we know it's real because we can feel it, breathe it, and experience it. Similarly, Allah has given us many signs around us — in nature, in the Al-Quran, and in our own experiences — that point to His existence. These signs strengthen our faith."

Raef paused, then asked, "Now, think about this: If everything were obvious — if everything were shown to us — would we still value our faith as much? Would we be as eager to seek the deeper truths of life, or would it just be another fact to accept, like the air we breathe?"

The teens sat quietly, some nodding, others still thinking. Sarah, who had been quiet so far, asked, "So, you're saying that faith is like a choice? It's something we work for, not just something that's handed to us?"

"Exactly," Brother Raef said. "Faith is a journey. It's not blind belief. It's a belief built on reflection, asking questions, seeking knowledge, and understanding the signs Allah has already given us. Look at the world around you — at the stars in the sky, the balance in nature, the miracles of life. These are all signs of Allah's existence."

Liam seemed thoughtful. "But what if some people never see those signs or never understand them?"

Raef nodded. "That's where the test comes in. Everyone has a different starting point on their journey. But the opportunity to seek and understand is available to everyone. Allah has sent messengers and scriptures to guide us, and He has made His signs clear to those who reflect on them. Some people may ignore these signs, and others may not understand them right away. But if someone is sincere in their search for truth, Allah promises to guide them."

Layla looked around at her friends, then back at Brother Raef. "But if we can't see Allah, how do we know we're on the right path?"

Raef's eyes softened. "The path to Allah is clear, Layla. It's not about seeing Him physically; it's about following the guidance He has provided. It's about living with kindness, justice, and righteousness. It's about striving to understand the Al-Quran, to act according to its teachings, and to call upon Allah with sincerity. Allah is closer to us than we can imagine, and He knows what's in our hearts."

Sarah, still uncertain, asked, "But what about people who doubt all of this? How can they believe if they don't see any proof?"

Raef looked at her, his voice calm and kind. "Doubt is part of the journey, Sarah. It's natural to question things. It's natural to search for answers. But the beauty of faith is that it's not about absolute certainty or evidence you can touch with your hands. It's about the peace you find when you open your heart to something greater, when you see the signs around you and in your life, and when you turn to Allah in times of need."

Brother Raef's voice grew even softer.

"Allah says in the Al-Quran, 'Say, 'My Lord, increase me in knowledge" (Chapter/Surah Ta-Ha: 20, Verse: 114).

The search for truth is a lifelong journey. It's not about proving everything all at once—it's about continually seeking, reflecting, and growing."

The room was silent for a moment as the teens absorbed what Raef had said. Though their doubts were still there, they felt lighter. The seeds of faith were beginning to take root, not because they had all the answers, but because they were starting to trust the process. They were beginning to understand that faith, like life itself, was a journey — not an immediate conclusion.

Brother Raef smiled. "The road may be long, and the questions may be many, but Allah promises that He is always near. Keep asking. Keep searching. And keep trusting."

"Food For Thought"

Q. 1. Why do you think Allah wants us to believe in Him from our hearts and not just because we see Him?

Q. 2. How can we recognize Allah's signs even though we can't see Him directly?

Q. 3. What do you think Brother Raef meant by saying that faith is a journey, not just blind belief?

Q. 4. How can someone who doubts everything still find peace and trust in Allah's guidance?

Q. 5. What are some ways we can strengthen our faith and trust the process of seeking truth?

"Seen or Unseen: How Well Did You Grasp It?"

Q. 1. What is the main reason Brother Raef gives for why Allah doesn't show Himself directly to people?

A. Because Allah is angry with humans

B. Because people would become scared

C. Because faith is meant to come from the heart and through reflection

D. Because it is forbidden to see Allah

Answer:.....?

Q. 2. Which analogy did Brother Raef use to help explain the concept of believing in Allah without seeing Him?

A. Believing in dreams

B. Air — we can't see it, but we experience it

C. The light of the sun

D. Solving a puzzle

Answer:.....?

Q. 3. What does the Quranic verse (Al-Quran 2:23) mentioned by Brother Raef challenge people to do?

A. To stop asking questions

B. To find Allah in the mountains

C. To produce a Chapter/Surah like the Quran if

they doubt its origin

D. To believe in everything without proof

Answer:....?

Q. 4. According to Brother Raef, how should someone respond when they experience doubt in their faith?

A. Ignore the doubt and pretend it's not there

B. Stop thinking and just follow what others say

C. Keep asking questions, seek knowledge, and reflect

D. Wait for someone else to guide them

Answer:....?

Q. 5. What does the verse from Al-Quran (20:114) remind us to do in our search for truth?

A. To worship only in the mosque

B. To avoid reading too many books

C. To pray five times a day

D. To ask Allah to increase our knowledge

Answer:....?

Part: 7

Living a Meaningful Life: Reflections and Decisions

As the evening came to a close, the group of teens sat around Brother Raef, their faces a blend of curiosity and deep thought. They had spent hours discussing profound questions about faith, life, and the afterlife. Now, Brother Raef felt it was time for one final thought that would stay with them long after the evening had ended.

"Every decision you make, every action you take, shapes the course of your life," he said calmly. "The beauty of it is that no matter where you are right now, or where you've been, you always have the power to change. You have the ability to return to what is right, seek forgiveness, and aim for something better."

The teens looked up, waiting for him to continue. Layla spoke first, her voice soft but sincere. "Brother Raef, how do we know if we're doing enough? How can we tell if our actions really matter in the grand scheme of things?"

Raef smiled gently.

"In the Al-Quran, Allah says, 'So whoever does an atom's weight of good will see it, and whoever does an atom's weight of evil will see it" *(Chapter/Surah Az-Zalzalah: 99, Verses: 7-8).*

This means that even the smallest good deed is seen by Allah. Whether it's a smile, a kind word, or helping someone in need, Allah sees it all. Every small act of kindness counts, no matter how insignificant it may seem."

Liam, who had been quiet for most of the evening, leaned forward. "But what if we mess up? What if we make mistakes?"

Raef nodded thoughtfully. "Everyone makes mistakes, Liam. It's part of being human. But don't let your mistakes define you. Islam teaches us about repentance — the chance to turn back to Allah and ask for His forgiveness. Allah is full of mercy, and He loves to forgive. No matter how far you've strayed, there is always a way back."

He looked around at the group, his eyes filled with compassion. "Repentance isn't just about asking for forgiveness; it's about choosing to change. It's about turning away from what is wrong and striving to do what is right. Each time you make that choice, you shape your future and your character."

"But how do we know we're on the right path?" Sarah asked, her voice filled with doubt. "There are so many choices in life. How do we know what's truly right?"

Raef smiled. "That's the beauty of life. Allah has given us guidance. We're not left to figure everything out on our own. Through the Al-Quran, the teachings of Prophet Muhammad (PBUH), and through our own hearts, we can find the direction we need. And if you feel lost or uncertain, remember this: the most important thing is to strive. Strive to do good, strive for truth, and strive to do what's right—that's what matters."

He paused, letting his words sink in. "And you don't have to do it alone. You've got friends, family, and a community to help guide you. But it's your decisions, your choices, that will define the person you become."

Layla looked at her hands, thinking deeply. "So, even if we don't have all the answers, we should just keep trying to do good and follow what we believe is right?"

Raef nodded. "Exactly. Life isn't about perfection. It's about growth. It's about striving to be better today than you were yesterday. And when you make a mistake, don't give up. Ask for forgiveness, learn from it, and keep going."

Liam spoke up again, his voice more determined. "I think I understand now. It's not about being perfect; it's about making the effort and doing the right thing, even when it's hard."

"Exactly, Liam," Raef said, smiling. "You're never too far gone to make a change. Every step you take toward goodness counts. The most important thing is to live consciously. Be mindful of your choices. Be mindful of your actions.

Allah says, "Indeed, Allah does not change the condition of a people until they change what is in themselves.' (Chapter/Surah Ar-Rad: 13, Verse: 11)."

Brother Raef stood up, signaling the end of their discussion. "Before we leave, remember this: Your life is in your hands. The choices you make today will shape the person you become tomorrow. Allah, in His mercy, has given you the opportunity to choose your path. Live with intention. Strive for good. Seek truth. And know that Allah is always watching, always guiding."

The teens sat quietly, reflecting on his words. A calm understanding filled the room. They realized that they had the power to shape their futures through their choices.

As they got ready to leave, Sarah turned to Brother Raef and asked one last question. "What's the best way to start living a meaningful life?"

Raef smiled warmly. "Start with sincerity. Begin with the intention to seek truth, to live righteously, and to help others. And always remember that every small act of goodness matters." Here the

Contemporary Questions and Answers-

How can I balance my faith with the pressures of society?

Raef answered thoughtfully, "Society may push you in many directions, but remember, Allah has given us clear guidance. When you face challenges, turn to the Al-Quran, the teachings of the Prophet (PBUH), and seek the support of your community. Stay true to what you know is right, even when it's hard."

What if I don't feel close to Allah? How can I strengthen my connection?

"It's okay to feel distant at times," Raef said with understanding. "Start small—make time for your prayers, even when it feels difficult. Read the Al-Quran with reflection, ask questions, seek knowledge, and surround yourself with good company. And remember, Allah is always closer to you than you realize."

What if I have doubts about my faith?

"Doubt is a part of seeking the truth," Raef reassured. "Keep asking questions and reflecting on Allah's signs. The Al-Quran says,

"Say, My Lord, increase me in knowledge" (Chapter/SurahTa-Ha: 20, Verse: 114).

Be patient, continue your search for answers, and trust that your faith will grow over time."

How can I be sure that the choices I'm making now are the right ones for my future?

"It's difficult to know everything for sure," Raef acknowledged. "But focus on what aligns with good character, kindness, and justice. Make decisions based on what you know is right, and trust in Allah's plan for you. Remember, every step you take toward goodness shapes your future."

How do I find purpose in life when everything seems confusing?

Raef smiled kindly. "Purpose comes from living with intention. Find what brings you peace, what connects you to others, and what helps you serve Allah's will. Whether it's helping others, learning, or being kind, your purpose will unfold as you strive for good."

What if I feel like I'm too far gone to make a change?

Raef gently reassured them, "No one is too far gone for Allah's mercy. You can always turn back, no matter your past.

The Al-Quran reminds us, "And your Lord is Forgiving, full of mercy" (Chapter/Surah Al-Kahf: 18,

Verse: 58). Repentance and change are always possible.

Conclusion: The Power of Choice

As the teens prepared to leave, they felt a newfound sense of clarity and peace. They understood that a meaningful life wasn't about being perfect; it was about striving for goodness, seeking truth, and making decisions that reflected their values. Every choice, big or small, mattered. And Allah's mercy and guidance were always there to help them grow.

As they left Brother Raef that evening, each teen carried with them a commitment to live a life of intention. They would continue to make mistakes, but they now knew that repentance and striving for what's right were the keys to shaping their future.

The story of their evening together would remain with them, a reminder that life is about growth, striving for good, and knowing that Allah's mercy is always there for those who seek it.

"Food For Thought"

Q. 1. What is the most important lesson you learned from Brother Raef's words?

Q. 2. How can you make small acts of kindness a part of your daily life?

Q. 3. How do you feel about the idea that making mistakes doesn't define you?

Q. 4. What steps can you take to strengthen your connection with Allah?

Q. 5. How will you make sure your choices reflect your values moving forward?

"Test Your Takeaway: What Did You Learn?"

Q. 1. What was Brother Raef's main message to the teens about living a meaningful life?

A. Life is about achieving success and avoiding failure

B. Living a meaningful life means striving for perfection

C. Life is about striving to do good, learning from mistakes, and seeking truth

D. Life is predetermined and cannot be changed

Answer:....?

Q. 2. According to the story, how does Islam view small acts of kindness?

A. They are insignificant in the grand scheme of life

B. Only large, noticeable deeds matter in faith

C. Small acts are recorded and rewarded by Allah

D. Kindness is only valuable during religious rituals

Answer:....?

Q. 3. What did Brother Raef say about making mistakes?

A. Mistakes cannot be undone and define our character

B. Everyone makes mistakes, and repentance allows us to grow and return to Allah

C. Only major sins need to be repented for

D. Mistakes mean we are not true believers

Answer:....?

Q. 4. How did Brother Raef suggest teens can stay on the right path when facing life's choices?

A. By following trends and societal expectations

B. By isolating themselves from the world

C. By using the Quran, teachings of the Prophet (PBUH), and self-reflection

D. By relying only on their feelings

Answer:....?

Q. 5. What final advice did Brother Raef give about beginning to live a meaningful life?

A. Focus on accumulating wealth and influence

B. Start with sincerity and small acts of goodness

C. Wait for the right time to change

D. Avoid making any decisions without full certainty

Answer:....?

Part: 8

Life Beyond Earth: Is There a Hereafter?

The group of teens gathered again in their usual spot, their curiosity buzzing after last week's discussion about angels. Tonight's topic was one that everyone wondered about but rarely discussed openly—the afterlife, or what happens after we die. As the evening sun set, Brother Raef began to speak.

"Last time, we talked about how angels record our actions. Tonight, let's explore a big question: What happens after we die?"

There was a murmur of surprise and curiosity. Sarah, always quick with her notebook, raised her hand. "I've heard so many different things. Some people say we just disappear when we die, and others talk about heaven and hell. But how do we really know what's true?"

Raef nodded thoughtfully. "Great question, Sarah. The Al-Quran gives us a clear picture of what happens after death. It talks about resurrection, accountability, and the eternal life to follow. For example,

In Chapter/Surah At-Takathur: 102, Verse: 8, Allah (SWT) says: "Then you will surely be asked that Day about pleasure."

This verse tells us that everything we enjoy in this world will be questioned, and we will be held accountable for how we used our blessings."

Liam, always the skeptic, leaned back with a grin. "But how do we know that's true? No one's come back to tell us what really happens after death."

Raef smiled gently, expecting this. "You're right, Liam. No one has come back to tell us, but think about this: there are many things in life we believe in without seeing them firsthand. For example, we trust that a seed will grow into a tree, even though we can't see the process right away. Why? Because the evidence is all around us. Similarly, the idea of the afterlife is supported by the Al-Quran, which has stayed the same for over 1,400 years and contains truths that even modern science is only now discovering. Isn't that something worth thinking about?"

Liam shrugged but didn't say anything.

Aisha, who had been thinking deeply, asked, "But why would there even be a resurrection? Why bring us back after we die?"

Raef's face softened. "That's an important question, Aisha. Allah created this life as a test, and the Hereafter is where the results of that test are shown.

In Chapter/Surah Al-Mulk: 67, Verse: 2, Allah says: "[He] who created death and life to test you [as to] which of you is best in deed."

Without the Hereafter, there would be no ultimate justice. Imagine if someone did terrible things in this life and faced no consequences. The Day of Judgment is the day when everyone will be held accountable, and no good or bad deed will go unnoticed."

Sarah nodded, understanding. "Okay, that makes sense. But how does resurrection even work? Our bodies decompose when we die. How can we be brought back?"

Raef pointed to a tree outside the window, its leaves swaying in the wind. "Look at that tree. In winter, it looks dead, right? But in spring, it blooms again. Allah brings life back to what seems lifeless. If Allah can revive a tree, then why would it be hard for Him to resurrect us?

In Chapter/Surah Yasin: 36, Verse: 79, Allah says: "He will give them life who produced them the first time; and He is, of all creation, Knowing."

Allah, who created us from nothing, can bring us back, no matter what state we're in."

Ahmad, who had been quiet until now, spoke up. "But why make the afterlife such a big deal? Can't we just live our lives and see what happens after death?"

Raef looked at him kindly. "That's a fair thought, Ahmad. But let me ask you this: If you were given an exam and didn't know what the questions would be, wouldn't you study just in case? The afterlife is like that exam. Allah has already given us the questions — how we live, how we treat others, and how we use the blessings He has given us. Ignoring the afterlife doesn't make it disappear. Preparing for it ensures that we're ready when the time comes."

Liam leaned forward, his curiosity starting to show. "But what if someone doesn't believe in all of this? Does that mean they automatically go to hell?"

Raef paused for a moment, carefully choosing his words. "It's not for me or anyone else to judge who goes where. That's Allah's decision. What we know for sure is that Allah is fair and just.

In Chapter/Surah An-Nisa: 4, Verse: 40, Allah says: "Indeed, Allah does not do injustice, [even] as much as an atom's weight."

Allah gives everyone the chance to seek the truth and choose their path. What matters is sincerity — whether you've truly searched for answers and lived your life with integrity."

Sarah, who had been listening carefully, spoke up. "But isn't it unfair that some people don't even know about Islam or the teachings of the Al-Quran? Do they get a fair chance?"

Raef smiled gently. "Another great question, Sarah. Allah knows everyone's heart and intentions. *In Chapter/Surah Al-Baqarah: 2, Verse: 286, Allah says: "Allah does not burden a soul beyond that it can bear."*

Allah judges everyone based on what they knew, what they were exposed to, and how they tried to live their lives. Those who never heard about Islam or had no opportunity to learn will not be judged in the same way as those who were given the message and rejected it."

The room fell silent for a moment as the teens thought about the answers. Raef leaned forward, his voice serious. "Let me leave you with this thought: If there's even the slightest chance that the Hereafter is real, doesn't it make sense to learn more about it? To prepare, just in case? After all, the stakes couldn't be higher — eternal happiness or eternal regret."

The teens exchanged glances. Each one of them was left with deep thoughts, the question of the

Hereafter lingering in their minds. As they left that evening, the conversation remained with them, sparking new questions and perhaps a deeper desire to uncover the truth.

"Food For Thought"

Q. 1. What happens after we die?

Q. 2. Why is there a Day of Judgment?

Q. 3. How can we prepare for the afterlife?

Q. 4. Why is faith important in believing in the unseen?

Q. 5. What lesson did you find most interesting from today's discussion?

Let's Enjoy Checking Our Reading Abilities!

Q. 1. What does Chapter/Surah Al-Mulk (67:2) teach us about the purpose of life and death?

A. To enjoy the world and its pleasures

B. To test which of us earns the most money

C. To test who among us does the best deeds

D. To show that life is temporary and meaningless

Answer:....?

Q. 2. According to Brother Raef, what makes belief in the afterlife reasonable even if we cannot see it?

A. It's just a traditional belief passed down

B. Scientific experiments prove it

C. The Al-Quran's teachings and observable examples from nature

D. People have come back to tell us about it

Answer:....?

Q. 3. What example did Raef use to explain the concept of resurrection after death?

A. A newborn baby growing up

B. The change of seasons from spring to summer

C. A tree that appears dead in winter but revives in spring

D. A student passing an exam

Answer:....?

Q. 4. What key concept is emphasized in chapter/Surah An-Nisa (4:40)?

A. Everyone will enter paradise eventually

B. Allah does not forgive major sins

C. Allah never acts unjustly, not even the weight of an atom

D. People are punished immediately after doing wrong

Answer:....?

Q. 5. Why did Raef compare the afterlife to an exam?

A. To show that life is a game with winners and losers

B. To suggest we should memorize all the answers

C. To emphasize that we should prepare in advance because the questions are known

D. To make the teens anxious about the future

Answer:....?

Part: 9

Paradise: Just a Fairy Tale?

The evening air was warm, and the scent of flowers drifted in from outside as Brother Raef gathered the teens for another discussion. Tonight, there was an energy in the room that felt different—curiosity mixed with skepticism. They were eager to dive into a subject many had heard of but perhaps never fully understood: Paradise.

"Alright, everyone," Brother Raef began. "Tonight, we're going to talk about Jannah, Paradise. I know it's a concept many of you have heard of, but I want to explore it with you in detail. Is it just a fairy tale, as some might say, or is there something deeper to it?"

Sarah, who was always quick to ask questions, raised her hand. "I've heard a lot about Jannah—gardens, rivers, palaces. It sounds like something out of a fantasy book. But how do we know it's real? It's hard to believe in something we can't see or touch."

Brother Raef nodded, understanding the doubt. "It's completely normal to question what we can't physically see, Sarah. But think about this: the Al-Quran doesn't describe Paradise in vague terms. It paints a picture that appeals to our senses, something we can imagine but also can't fully comprehend.

Allah describes Jannah as "gardens of perpetual residence." (Chapter/Surah Ar-Rad: 13, Verse:: 23).

These gardens are beyond anything we've seen, a place of peace, beauty, and endless joy."

Ahmad raised an eyebrow and asked, "Gardens? How's that even a reward? It seems pretty simple. What's so special about that?"

Brother Raef smiled, sensing that Ahmad's question was more about the concept of reward than the physical garden itself. "Good question, Ahmad. When we think of rewards, we often think of material things—money, cars, status. But in Paradise, the rewards are far beyond that. It's a place where we're free from pain, stress, and sadness. Imagine a world where there's no pain, no suffering, and no worries. Everything is perfect. We can be with the people we love and enjoy eternal peace."

Liam, who had been quiet, leaned forward. "But if it's so perfect, why would Allah reward people so lavishly? Doesn't that sound too good to be true? Why would God/Allah (SWT) give such extravagant rewards for the things we do in this life?"

Brother Raef paused for a moment, letting the question hang in the air. "That's a great point, Liam. It might seem like an exaggeration, right? But think about it this way: what does Allah promise in the Al-Quran? That He's the most merciful, the most generous. Every good deed we do, no matter how small, is rewarded by Him. And the reward in Paradise? That's the ultimate.

In Chapter/Surah Al-Insan: 76, Verse 11, it says: "And He will protect them from the evil of that Day and give them radiance and happiness."

Aisha, who had been thinking deeply, spoke up, "So, are you saying that what we do here, how we live our lives, determines the reward we get in the Hereafter?"

"Exactly," Raef said. "Everything we do here matters. Every small act of kindness, every time we control our anger, every moment we choose what is right instead of what is easy—all of those choices shape our future. In Chapter/Surah Al-Imran: 3, Verse: 133, Allah says: 'And hasten to forgiveness from your Lord and a Paradise as wide as the heavens and earth, prepared for the righteous.' This is not a fairy tale, Aisha. It's a promise, and it's based on how we live our lives here."

Sarah furrowed her brow. "But if Allah rewards people so generously, what about those who don't believe in Him or do bad things? What happens to them?"

Brother Raef's expression became gentle, but his words were firm. "It's important to understand that Allah's justice is perfect. Those who choose to do wrong and refuse to seek forgiveness will face the consequences. In Chapter/Surah Al-Bayyina: 98, Verse: 6, it says: 'Indeed, those who disbelieve and do not do righteous deeds—those are the worst of creatures.' But remember, Allah is also the most merciful. If someone sincerely repents, He forgives. So, the choice is ours. We can choose to seek His mercy, and He promises Paradise for those who do."

Liam's face softened. "So, it's not just about what we believe, but how we act too?"

Raef nodded. "Exactly, Liam. In Jannah, we will be reunited with our loved ones—our parents, our spouses, even our children. It's a place where we don't have to worry about anything. It's all about peace and happiness."

Aisha looked thoughtful. "But how do we know the descriptions of Jannah in the Al-Quran are real? Why should we believe them?"

Raef smiled gently. "Great question. The Al-Quran wasn't written by a human. It was revealed by Allah to Prophet Muhammad (SAW). And it speaks of things that no one in the time of the Prophet could have known about. The beauty, the rivers, the gardens—all of these are beyond human imagination, which is why Allah describes them in the Al-Quran. But even if we can't fully understand it, we trust in the One who created it. Just like we trust in the things we can't see in this world—like gravity or electricity—we believe in the unseen because of our trust in Allah."

As the discussion continued, the room was filled with a sense of quiet contemplation. The teens had questions, doubts, and some of them even felt a spark of belief beginning to grow. As the night drew to a close, Brother Raef left them with one final thought.

"Paradise is not a fairy tale, my friends. It's real. And it's waiting for those who strive for it. The road may not always be easy, but remember: every step we take in the right direction brings us closer to that eternal garden."

"Food For Thought"

Q. 1. What is the main message Brother Raef is trying to share about Paradise?

Q. 2. How does believing in Paradise affect how we live our lives today?

Q. 3. Why is it important to act kindly and seek forgiveness, according to Brother Raef?

Q. 4. What do you think makes the idea of Jannah different from a fairy tale?

Q. 5. How does trusting in Allah help us believe in things we can't see, like Paradise?

Let's Have Fun Testing Our Reading Skills!

Q. 1. What does Brother Raef say is the true reward of Paradise (Jannah)?

A. Gold and silver palaces

B. Being free from pain, stress, and sadness

C. Endless fame and fortune

D. Living like kings and queens forever

Answer:.....?

Q. 2. According to the discussion, what does the Al-Quran say about Paradise in Chapter/Surah Al-Imran (3:133)?

A. It is only for those who never sin

B. It is as small as a village

C. It is as wide as the heavens and the earth, prepared for the righteous

D. It is a temporary place of rest

Answer:.....?

Q. 3. What is Brother Raef's response to the idea that Paradise is just a fairy tale?

A. He agrees and says it's symbolic

B. He explains that the Quran gives detailed, meaningful descriptions and it's a promise from Allah

C. He says it's up to each person to decide

D. He says we should believe it only if we want to

Answer:....?

Q. 4. Why is it important to act kindly and seek forgiveness, according to Brother Raef?

A. Because we want to impress others

B. Because it helps us become rich in this life

C. Because our actions in this life determine our reward in the Hereafter

D. Because everyone else does it

Answer:....?

Q. 5. What does Brother Raef compare believing in Paradise to?

A. Believing in fairy tales

B. Trusting historical stories

C. Believing in things like gravity or electricity – we don't see them, but we trust they exist

D. Imagining stories from books

Answer:....?

Part: 10

The Reality of Jahannam (Hellfire)

As the evening sky darkened, the teens gathered in the cozy room, the soft glow of the lights reflecting a serious mood. Brother Raef could sense the solemn atmosphere; tonight's topic would be tough, but important. They needed to talk about Jahannam — the Hellfire — and the balance between Allah's mercy and justice.

"Tonight, we'll discuss something that may be hard to hear," Brother Raef began softly. "It's about Jahannam. Many people struggle to understand why Hell exists when we also talk about Allah's mercy. But it's a reality we have to face, because just as Allah rewards those who do good, He also holds accountable those who choose to do wrong."

The room went silent, the teens paying close attention to his words.

"First, let me remind you of something important," Raef continued. "Allah is the most merciful, and His mercy is limitless. He gives us countless chances to repent and seek forgiveness for our mistakes. But He is also just. When someone repeatedly chooses to do wrong, when they reject His guidance and refuse to change, it's only fair that they face the consequences."

Sarah raised her hand. "But wait, Brother Raef… if Allah is so merciful, why does He punish anyone? Why not just forgive everyone?"

Raef nodded, understanding her concern. "That's a great question, Sarah. It's important to know that Allah's mercy is beyond what we can even imagine. But mercy doesn't mean there are no consequences for our actions. Imagine if someone hurts another person — they should face the consequences, right? It wouldn't be fair if they just got away with it."

Liam, who had been listening carefully, spoke up. "So, you're saying that Hell is for people who've done really bad things?"

Raef looked at him thoughtfully. "Yes, Liam. But more importantly, it's for those who reject Allah's guidance. Allah doesn't punish anyone without reason. He gives us all a lifetime to repent, to turn back to Him, and to seek His forgiveness. But if someone refuses all of that and chooses to live a life of disbelief, that leads to consequences."

Aisha, still unsure, frowned. "But how bad is Hell? I mean, we hear a lot about the fire, but how can we really understand it?"

Brother Raef sighed. "It's hard for us to fully understand the punishment of Hell because we've never experienced anything like it. Allah describes it in the Al-Quran, but we can't grasp the depth of the pain and suffering.

In Chapter/Surah An-Naba: 78, Verses: 21-22 Allah says, "Indeed, Hell has been lying in wait for the transgressors, a place of return."

It's a place of unimaginable torment for those who choose to reject the truth.

Sarah, still concerned, asked, "So, if someone doesn't believe in God/Allah (SWT) or does bad things, are they going to Hell?"

Raef paused before answering. "Let's think about it this way, Sarah. It's not just about one mistake or one wrong belief. It's about rejecting the truth Allah has given us. It's about choosing to live without considering the consequences. Everyone makes mistakes, but Allah gives us a chance to make things right. He says in the Al-Quran,

"Say, O My servants who have harmed yourselves by your own actions, do not despair of Allah's mercy. Allah forgives all sins; He is truly the Most Forgiving, Most Merciful" (Chapter/Surah Az-Zumar: 39, Verse: 53).

Liam raised an eyebrow. "So, if we repent and ask for forgiveness, we can avoid Hell?"

"Exactly," Raef said. "That's the beauty of Allah's mercy. If we turn to Him sincerely, He will forgive us, no matter what we've done. As long as we ask for forgiveness, He will show mercy."

Aisha, with a serious tone, asked, "What about people who don't believe in God/Allah (SWT) at all? What happens to them?"

Raef paused, understanding the weight of the question. "This is tough. Allah has given us guidance through His messengers, the Al-Quran, and our conscience. If someone knowingly rejects all of that, if they choose disbelief, there are consequences. But we don't know what's in anyone's heart except Allah. We can't judge others. What's important is that we focus on our own actions and strive to live right, seeking Allah's forgiveness."

Ahmad, who had been quiet, spoke up. "So, you're saying it's never too late for any of us to change? That we can still avoid Hell?"

Brother Raef smiled warmly. "Yes, Ahmad. It's never too late as long as we are alive. Allah is always ready to forgive us, but we have to take the first step. We need to turn to Him, try our best to live right, and ask for His mercy."

The room fell silent as the teens processed the gravity of the conversation. Raef could see their understanding deepening, piece by piece.

"Remember," Brother Raef said gently, "Allah's justice is fair, but His mercy is vast. Our job is to strive to be better, to seek forgiveness, and to always remember that Allah is watching over us, guiding us toward the right path."

The teens sat quietly, reflecting on what they had learned. Brother Raef had opened their eyes to the delicate balance between mercy and justice. As the evening came to an end, he left them with one final thought:

"Paradise is waiting for those who strive, and Jahannam is there for those who reject. We each have a choice. The best thing we can do is choose the path that leads to Allah's mercy."

"Food For Thought"

Q. 1. How does Brother Raef explain the balance between Allah's mercy and justice?

Q. 2. Why is it important to seek forgiveness from Allah, according to the discussion?

Q. 3. What does Brother Raef say about the possibility of changing and avoiding Hell?

Q. 4. How does Allah's mercy impact our actions and decisions in life?

Q. 5. What lesson can we learn from the conversation about choosing the right path in life?

Let's Check Our Reading and Understanding Abilities

Q. 1. What key message did Brother Raef share about the existence of Jahannam (Hell)?

A. It is a place created to scare people into worship.
B. It exists only for non-believers.
C. It is a consequence for those who knowingly reject Allah's guidance.
D. It is temporary for everyone.

Answer:.....?

Q. 2. According to Brother Raef, what is the main condition for receiving Allah's mercy?

A. Fasting during Ramadan only.
B. Memorizing the entire Quran.
C. Sincerely repenting and asking for forgiveness.
D. Never making any mistakes.

Answer:.....?

Q. 3. How did Brother Raef describe Allah's mercy compared to His justice?

A. Allah's mercy is only for Muslims, not for others.

B. Allah's mercy cancels out His justice.

C. Allah's mercy is vast, but justice ensures fairness for all actions.

D. Justice always comes before mercy.

Answer:....?

Q. 4. What example did Brother Raef use to help the teens understand the need for consequences?

A. A story from the Hadith.

B. Someone hurting another person and facing justice.

C. A story of a Prophet.

D. A parable about a fire.

Answer:....?

Q. 5. What message did Brother Raef leave the teens with at the end of the discussion?

A. Everyone is already destined for either Hell or Heaven.

B. Only scholars and saints go to Paradise.

C. We all have a choice, and we should strive for Allah's mercy.

D. Fear is the only way to stay on the right path.

Answer:....?

Attention!

Al-Quran is the final Divine Book revealed by God. Prior to the Quran, other Divine Scriptures were sent, including the **Torah, Zabur,** and **Injil** (Bible). All these books carry the voice and message of God. Ultimately, God revealed the *Al-Quran* as the universal and eternal constitution for humanity.

Over the past 1450 years, educators, researchers, and scholars around the world have not been able to identify a single error or contradiction in the *Al-Quran*. While some individuals have claimed that it requires changes or updates, God has addressed such claims within the *Al-Quran* itself by issuing a divine challenge: to produce even a single *Chapter/Surah* like it (Al-Baqarah, 2:23). This challenge remains active to this day, and no one has been able to meet it — nor will anyone be able to until the end of time.

The term **Surah** refers to a chapter in the *Al-Quran*. For example, the first Surah is called *Al-Fatihah* and the second is *Al-Baqarah*. The Quran contains a total of **114 Surahs (Chapters)**. Each Surah is composed of multiple verses, known as **Ayahs**. For the sake of clarity and ease of reference in this book, Quranic citations are provided using the format: *Surah name: verse number*. For example, *Al-Fatihah, 1:1* refers to *Surah Al-Fatihah, :1, verse 1*.

Dear readers, please note: if there are any mistakes in the explanation or interpretation in this book, they are entirely my own — due to my limited knowledge or understanding. However, the verses of the *Al-Quran* are absolutely free from error.

Thank you.

"Answers to the MCQs"

Part: One

Reflections of the Heart: What Did You Take In?

Q. 1. Why did Brother Raef share the story about footprints in the desert?

Answer: A

Q. 2. What does Surah Infitar (82:10-12) say about angels?

Answer: C

Q. 3. How did Brother Raef describe the concept of faith?

Answer: B

Q. 4. How did the teens initially react to the idea of angels recording their actions?

Answer: C

Q. 5. What was Brother Raef's main message at the end of the session?

Answer: D

Part: Two

Comprehension Check: Exploring Belief and Meaning

Q. 1. What does the verse from Surah Al-Hadid (57:4) emphasize about Allah?

Answer: B

Q. 2. How did Brother Raef describe Allah's presence to help the teens understand it?

Answer: C

Q. 3. According to Surah Al-An'am (6:103), why can't we see Allah?

Answer: D

Q. 4. Why did Brother Raef compare Allah's watchfulness to parents watching a school play?

Answer: B

Q. 5. What message does Surah Az-Zumar (39:53) convey?

Answer: C

Part: Three

Think Fast, Reflect Deep: What's Your Take?

Q. 1. According to Surah Al-Infitar (82:10-12), what is the primary role of the Kiraman Katibin?

Answer: A. To record all actions of humans

Q. 2. How does Raef explain the ability of angels to record everything we do?

Answer: C. By comparing them to modern devices that track data

Q. 3. Why, according to Raef, are humans not shown angels during their lifetime?

Answer: B. Because it would remove the test of faith

Q. 4. What is the significance of Surah Az-Zalzalah (99:7-8) as discussed in the story?

Answer: C. It emphasizes that even the smallest deeds are recorded.

Q. 5. What analogy does Raef use to help Ahmad understand the existence of angels?''

Answer: D. Gravity.

Part: Four

Challenge Yourself: What Do You Remember?

Q. 1. According to Brother Raef, what is the main purpose of our creation as mentioned in the Quran?

Answer: C. To worship Allah

Q. 2. What does Brother Raef explain about the meaning of worship in Islam?

Answer: C. It includes all actions done to please Allah

Q. 3. How did Brother Raef respond to the question about people who are kind but don't believe in Allah?

Answer: B. He emphasized that good deeds without belief miss the core purpose

Q. 4. What does Surah Al-Baqarah, verse 177, highlight as the foundation of righteous

Answer: C. Belief in Allah and living by His guidance

Q. 5. According to the discussion, how can Muslims help others find their purpose in life?

Answer: C. By living with faith and showing good actions

Part: Five

Faith in Focus: Check Your Understanding

Q. 1. What does Brother Raef say about Allah's knowledge and our free will?

Answer: C

Q. 2. According to Al-Quran 4:79, what is the source of the evil that befalls us?

Answer: A

Q. 3. How does Brother Raef explain our reaction to events we cannot control, like accidents?

Answer: C

Q. 4. Why does Brother Raef compare Allah's knowledge to a teacher knowing how a student will perform?

Answer: D

Q. 5. What does using our free will wisely mean in the context of accountability?

Answer: C

Part: Six

Seen or Unseen: How Well Did You Grasp It?

Q. 1. What is the main reason Brother Raef gives for why Allah doesn't show Himself directly to people?

Answer: C. Because faith is meant to come from the heart and through reflection

Q. 2. Which analogy did Brother Raef use to help explain the concept of believing in Allah without seeing Him?

Answer: B. Air—we can't see it, but we experience it

Q. 3. What does the Quranic verse (Al-Quran 2:23) mentioned by Brother Raef challenge people to do?

Answer: C. To produce a surah like the Quran if they doubt its origin

Q. 4. According to Brother Raef, how should someone respond when they experience doubt in their faith?

Answer: C. Keep asking questions, seek knowledge, and reflect

Q. 5. What does the verse from Al-Quran (20:114) remind us to do in our search for truth?

Answer: D. To ask Allah to increase our knowledge

Part: Seven

Test Your Takeaway: What Did You Learn?

Q. 1. What was Brother Raef's main message to the teens about living a meaningful life?

Answer: C. Life is about striving to do good, learning from mistakes, and seeking truth

Q. 2. According to the story, how does Islam view small acts of kindness?

Answer: C. Small acts are recorded and rewarded by Allah

Q. 3. What did Brother Raef say about making mistakes?

Answer: B. Everyone makes mistakes, and repentance allows us to grow and return to Allah

Q. 4. How did Brother Raef suggest teens can stay on the right path when facing life's choices?

Answer: C. By using the Quran, teachings of the Prophet (PBUH), and self-reflection.

Q. 5. What final advice did Brother Raef give about beginning to live a meaningful life?

Answer: B. Start with sincerity and small acts of goodness

Part: Eight

Let's Enjoy Checking Our Reading Abilities!

Q. 1. What does Surah Al-Mulk (67:2) teach us about the purpose of life and death?

Answer: C

Q. 2. According to Brother Raef, what makes belief in the afterlife reasonable even if we cannot see it?

Answer: C

Q. 3. What example did Raef use to explain the concept of resurrection after death?

Answer: C

Q. 4. What key concept is emphasized in Surah An-Nisa (4:40)?

Answer: C

Q. 5. Why did Raef compare the afterlife to an exam?

Answer: C

Part: Nine

Let's Have Fun Testing Our Reading Skills!

Q. 1. What does Brother Raef say is the true reward of Paradise (Jannah)?

Answer: B

Q. 2. According to the discussion, what does the Al-Quran say about Paradise in Surah Al-Imran (3:133)?

Answer: C

Q. 3. What is Brother Raef's response to the idea that Paradise is just a fairy tale?

Answer: B

Q. 4. Why is it important to act kindly and seek forgiveness, according to Brother Raef?

Answer: C

Q. 5. What does Brother Raef compare believing in Paradise to?

Answer: C

Part: Ten

Let's Check Our Reading and Understanding Abilities

Q. 1. What key message did Brother Raef share about the existence of Jahannam (Hell)?

Answer: C

Q. 2. According to Brother Raef, what is the main condition for receiving Allah's mercy?

Answer: C

Q. 3. How did Brother Raef describe Allah's mercy compared to His justice?

Answer: C

Q. 4. What example did Brother Raef use to help the teens understand the need for consequences?

Answer: B

Q. 5. What message did Brother Raef leave the teens with at the end of the discussion?

Answer: C